Oo Pp Qq Rr Ss Tt Uu Vv Ww Xx Yy Zz

School!

Full of Poems

by Dee Lillegard

illustrated by Don Carter

ALFRED A. KNOPF
New York

School
Wakes up early.
Just can't wait
to see who's coming.
Don't be late!

New Shoes

They stand at the door,
too shy to walk.
They have tongues,
but they don't talk . . .

Cubbies
Sad when empty.
When filled,
thrilled!

AMY

JACK

Hook

Hurry!
If you give him a minute,
he'll grab your jacket
. . . with *you* in it!

Teacher's Desk

Impressively large.
She's in charge!

Pencil

Wiggles and squiggles a scary face.
Then flips himself over—
Erase! Erase!

Paper

What's he hiding?
What's he about?
He needs your hand
to draw him out . . .

Crayon

Starts out tall
with a fine pointed head.
Never grows up . . .
grows *down* instead.

Scissors

Open shut
Open shut
A snippy pair,
they're quick to cut.

Glue

Stick with me,
says Glue with a grin,
and I'll stick with you . . .
through thick and thin.

Letters

They stand in line from A to Z,
longing to be wild and free,
to fly away like breezy birds . . .
in flocks of *words!*

Wastebasket

Feed me, feed me!
Yum yum yum . . .
Toss your tidbits
into my tum!

Calendar

January, February, March . . .
Monday, Tuesday, too.
Months and days of the week
he'll proudly display for you.

Swings

They hang around,
stare at the sky . . .
wait to be sat on
so they can *fly!*

Fence

Stands guard . . . all day.
Wishes he could run and play.
Loves it when kids come his way.

Slide

Slippery slithery
Slide says, *Go!*
This is no time to be shy
or slow.

Rug
Likes nothing more
than snoozing
on the floor.
Listen closely.
Hear him snore?

Clock

Watches all the time.
Worries, *Am I late?*
Always on the move.
Impatient. Won't wait.

Books

Closed shut . . .
Secrets to hide?
Or waiting for you to say
Open wide!

Fountain

Gushes and bubbles
when you turn her on.
Hangs her head quietly
after you're gone.

Window

Shows us if it's sunny,
or if the weather's drippy-runny,
or if the clouds are acting *funny* . . .

Numbers

1's a stick.
2's a birdie.
3 is bubbly.
4 is sturdy.
If fidgety 5
gets out of line,
down go 6,
7, 8, 9!

Table
Loves a mess.
Oh yes!

Paintbrush
When paint gets in his hair,
Brush creates a scene,
swishing yellow, swashing red,
splashing blue and green.

Clay
A squooshy mooshy
shape-changer.
Pick her up
and re-arrange her!

Easel

Easily stands for hours,
holding up *mountains* . . .
or flowers.

Chair

Doesn't mind
your behind.
Prefers your seat
to shoes or feet.

Beads

Scattery chattery,
wondering whether
they want to be strung
on a string all together.

Blocks

They mumble, fumble,
climb from their jumble.
Up they scramble!
Then grumble when they
tumble . . .

Truck

Vroom! Vroom!
Across the room . . .
Look out, feet.
Here I zoom!

Puzzle

Falls to pieces . . .
gets mixed up that way.
Hopes you will put him
together today.

Puppet

Give me your hand; your voice, too.
Then see what a hollow-head fellow
can do . . .

Costume Box

Opens up and spills out
capes, scarves, a pig's snout,
a clown's nose and floppy feet,
witch's wand and ghostly sheet,
wigs and hats of every hue . . .
Get ready to be someone new!

Drum

Rum-tum! Rum-tum!
Bang-a-bang-a-bam!
A happy-to-be-noisy person . . .
that's what I am!

Xylophone

Hammer me. It's okay.
It's my favorite way to play.

Tambourine

Shake-a-shake-a-shake!
I love the sound I make!

Door
Opens wide
to let us know,
It's time to go,
It's time to go.

Bye-bye, School!

A smile.
A sigh.
School waves
Bye-bye . . .

For the Bryants,
Charles and Debra, Chaz
and Eli—and their
California cousins.

—D.L.

To my heroes:
Maurice Sendak, Tomie
dePaola, Dan Yaccarino,
Lane Smith, William Joyce,
and Curious George.

—D.C.

THIS IS A BORZOI BOOK PUBLISHED BY ALFRED A. KNOPF
Text copyright © 2001 by Dee Lillegard
Illustrations copyright © 2001 by Donald J. Carter
All rights reserved under International and Pan-American Copyright Conventions. Published in the United States
of America by Alfred A. Knopf, a division of Random House, Inc., New York, and simultaneously in Canada by
Random House of Canada Limited, Toronto. Distributed by Random House, Inc., New York.
KNOPF, BORZOI BOOKS, and the colophon are registered trademarks of Random House, Inc.

www.randomhouse.com/kids

Library of Congress Cataloging-in-Publication Data
Lillegard, Dee.
Hello school! : a classroom of poems / by Dee Lillegard ; illustrated by Don Carter.
p. cm.
1. Education, Preschool–Juvenile poetry. 2. Kindergarten–Juvenile poetry.
3. Schools–Juvenile poetry. 4. Children's poetry, American.
[1. Kindergarten–Poetry. 2. Schools–Poetry. 3. American poetry.]
I. Carter, Don, 1958– ill. II. Title.
PS3562.I4557 H45 2001
811'.54–dc21
00-059923
ISBN 0-375-81020-X (trade)
ISBN 0-375-91020-4 (lib. bdg.)
Printed in the United States of America
July 2001
10 9 8 7 6 5 4 3 2 1
First Edition